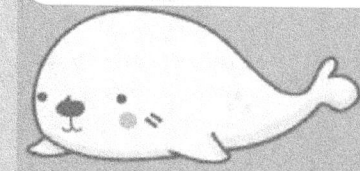

koala

polar bear

Gorilla

sea lion

FOX

first 100 animals

parrot

seahorse

ladybug

tiger

dolphin

Hornbill

Owl

Farm Animals

dog

cat

COW

sheep

rabbit

duck

chicken

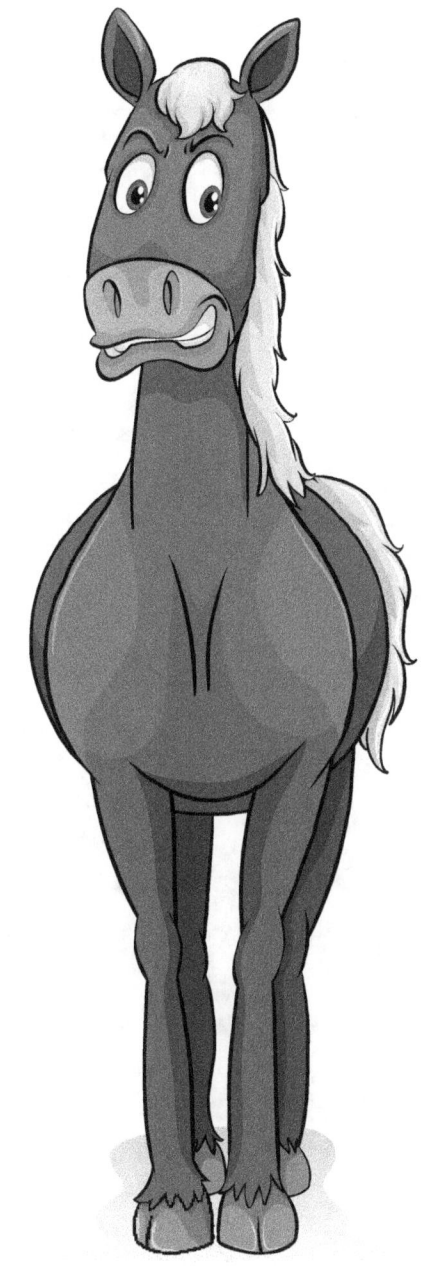

horse

pig

turkey

donkey

goat

guinea pig

hen

mouse

llama

Forest Animals

squirrel

snail

chameleon

deer

raccoon

beaver

weasel

hedgehog

koala

sloth

groundhog

anteater

panda

bear

wombat

mole

woodpecker

boar

Jungle Animals

lion

monkey

tiger

elephant

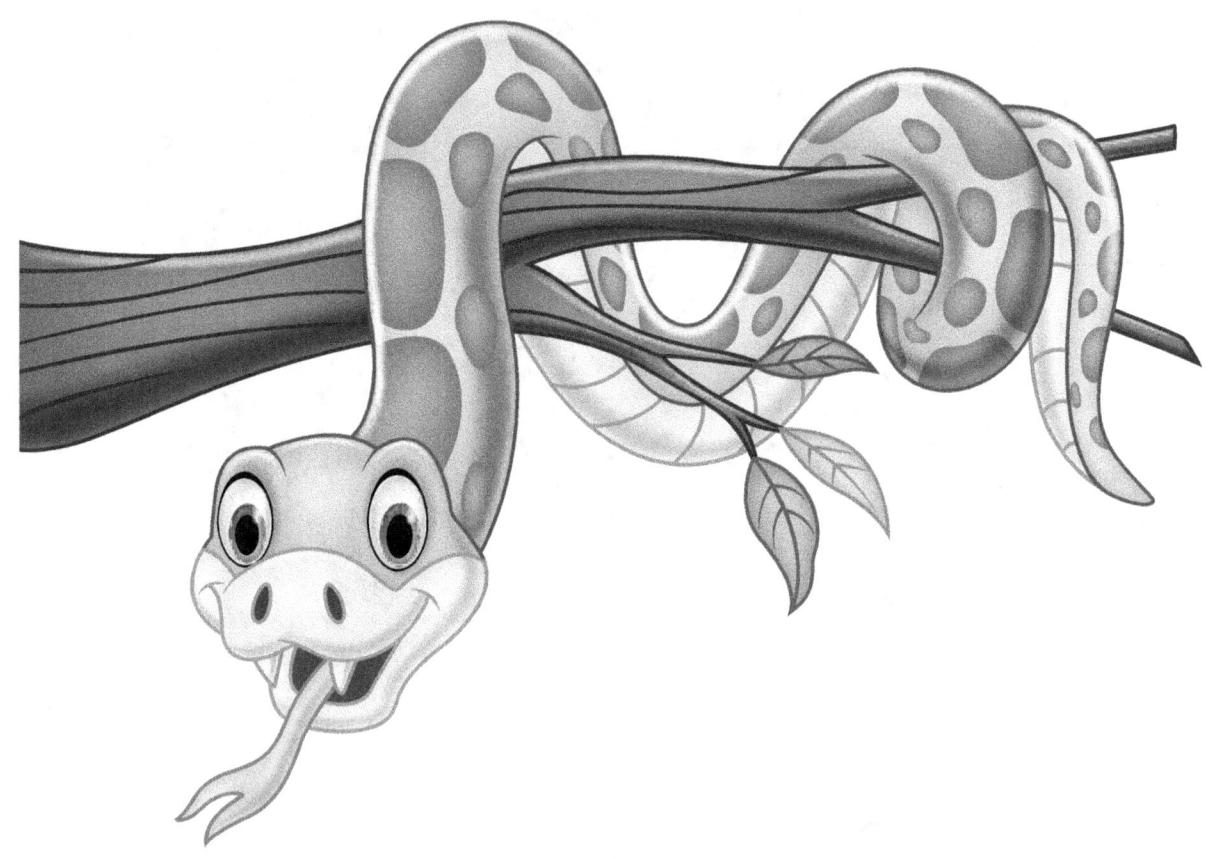

snake

bat

leopard

parrot

eagle

cockatoo

orangutan

Gorilla

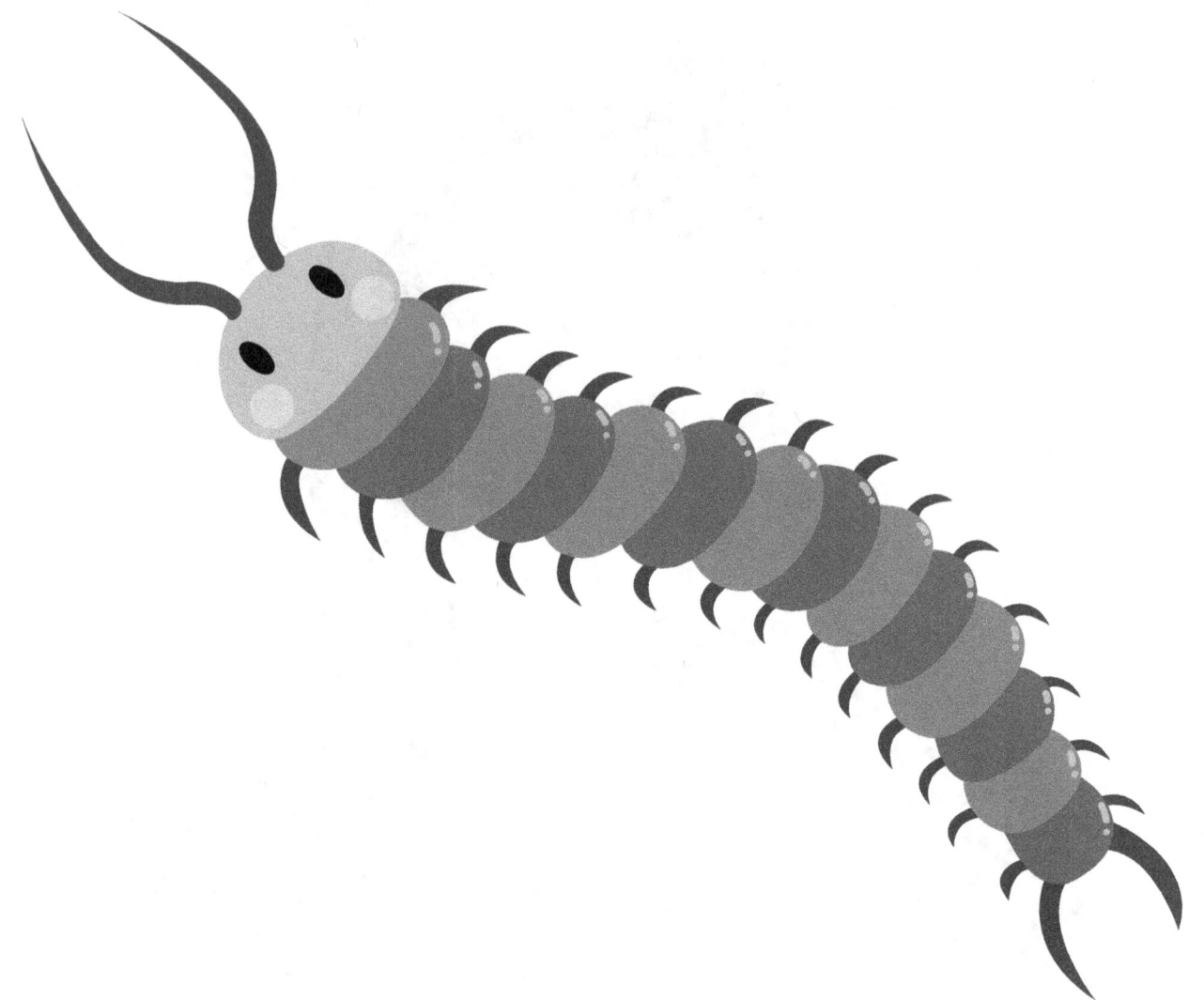

centipede

Owl

crow

Hornbill

hummingbird

Aquatic Animals

turtle

octopus

frog

whale

crab

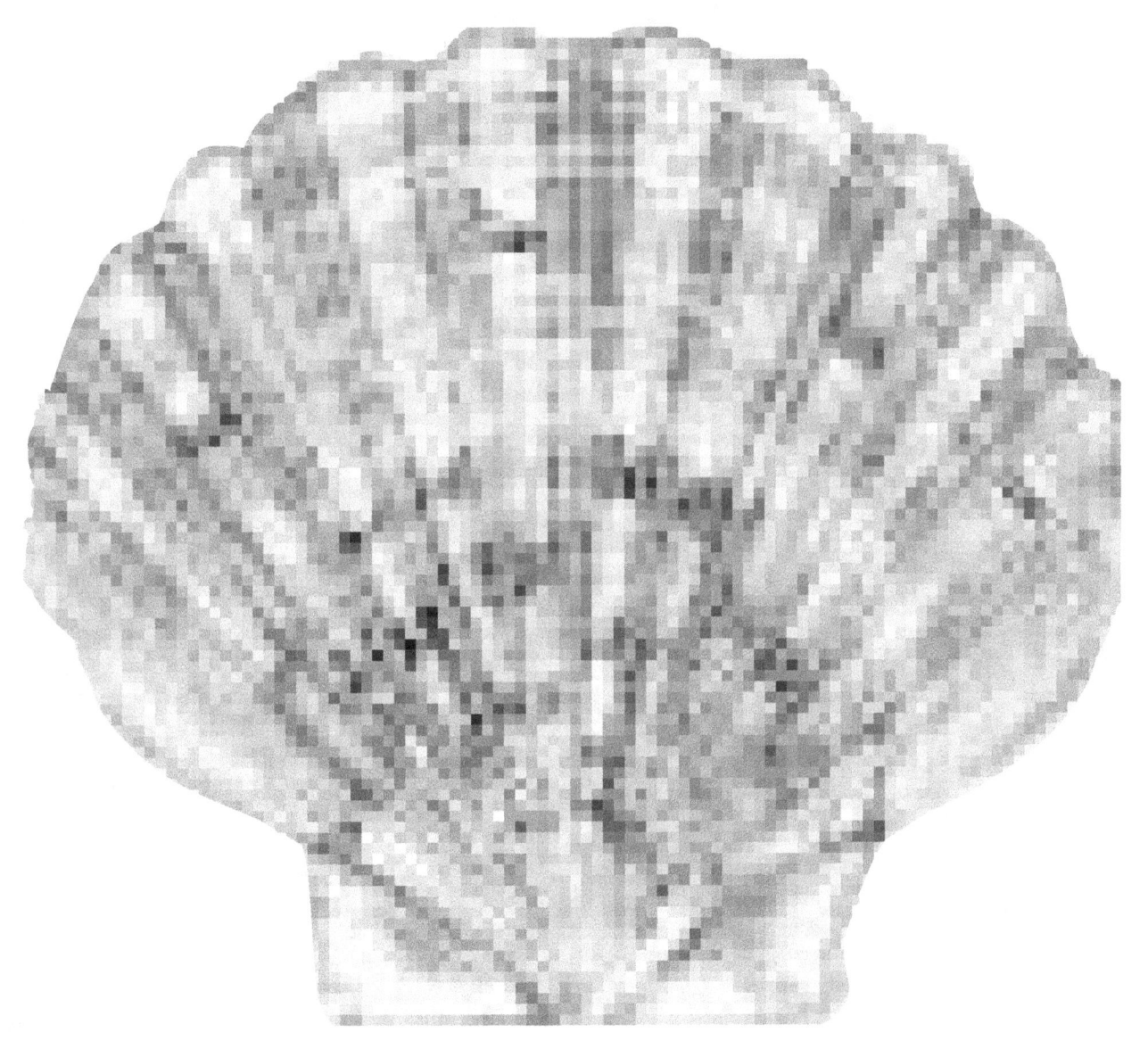

shell

fish

lobster

shark

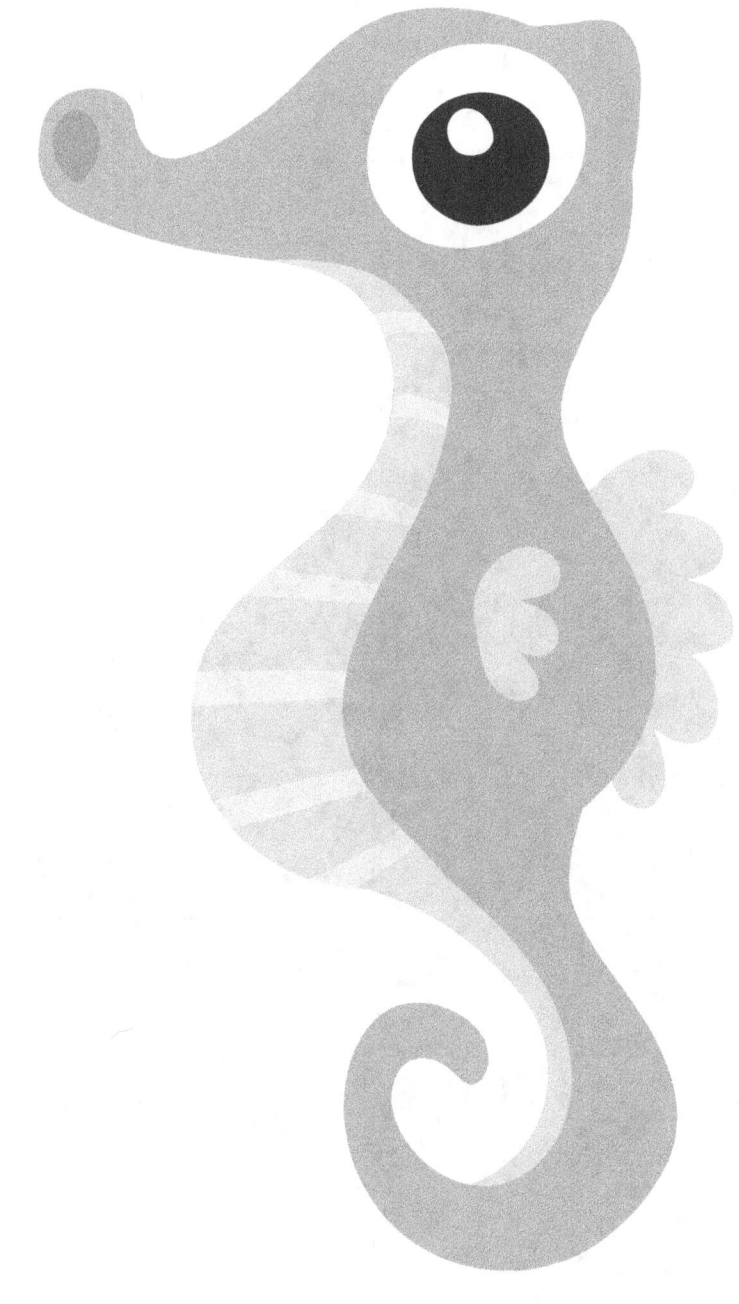

seahorse

hippopotamus

squid

shrimp

dolphin

starfish

alligator

jellyfish

Desert Animals

FOX

wilddog

Zebra

Meerkat

camel

giraffe

scorpion

hyena

impala

Kangaroo

ostrich

vulture

Armadillo

Arctic Animals

polar
bear

seal

reindeer

walrus

sea otter

orca

penguin

sea lion

Moose

Insects

bee

ant

butterfly

cockroach

beetle

grasshopper

dragonfly

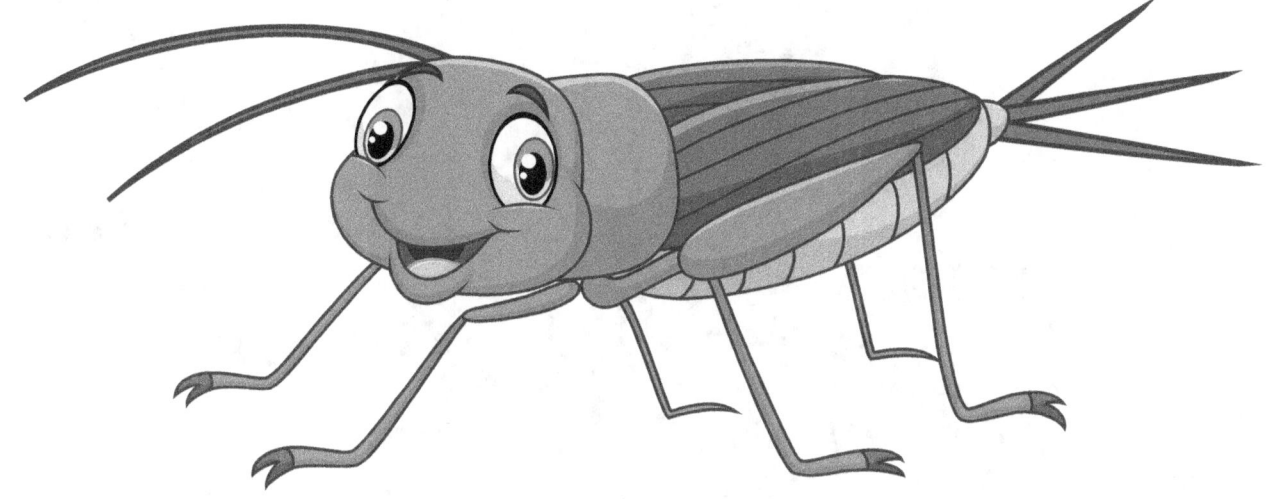

cricket

spider

ladybug